The Art of Unlearning

Volume V

TOP EXPERTS SHARE
PERSONAL STORIES ABOUT
FINDING LIGHT THROUGH THE
DARKNESS

DIVYA PAREKH & LISA MARIE PEPE

The Art of UnLearning: Top Experts Share Personal
Stories on Finding The Light Through The Darkness

Copyright © 2023

GET PUBLISHED

To receive your free gift and see how you, too, can become a published author, email us as
info@getpublishedwithus.com

CONTENTS

DEDICATION

This book is dedicated to women entrepreneurs across the globe. We are also thrilled to share that the proceeds of the sales of this book (minus our expenses) will be donated to Kiva. Kiva.org is an international non-profit founded in 2005 and based in San Francisco, with a mission to connect people through lending to alleviate poverty.

Kiva celebrates and supports people looking to create a better future for themselves, their families, and their communities. By giving as little as $25 to Kiva, anyone can help a borrower start or grow a business, go to school, access clean energy, or realize their potential. For some, it's a matter of survival; for others, it's the fuel for a lifelong ambition (Referenced from https://www.kiva.org/work-with-us/fellows).

The profits of this book (minus our expenses) go straight to Kiva, and once there, 100% of every dollar goes to funding loans. Kiva covers administrative costs primarily through voluntary donations, as well as through support from grants and sponsors.

We can't tell you how excited we are to be supporting lives and dreams in so many lives because of this book!

Divya Parekh and Lisa Marie Pepe

INTRODUCTION

Life is a harrowing journey where everyone experiences unique turns and roadblocks. We all encounter setbacks and dead ends. How we overcome those obstacles is what defines us!

In this book are the experiences of five gifted women and their stories about what life put in front of them. While the circumstances were different, as were their solutions, they had in common: each woman charted their course as they searched for their way out of the darkness where they found themselves. Now they want to share their personal stories with other women to inspire others.

The stories follow a general theme of women facing tragedies that seemed overwhelming initially, but they were able to navigate their way to their light. While these women now work actively today with other women in various ways, they believe their stories can serve as a guide for others. Often, when we know we are not alone in what we are facing, we find the inner courage to press ahead because we know others were successful.

You might see yourself in one story or pieces of yourself in all nine. Take out of these stories what you find beneficial to your situation. As each of these women shows, it takes perseverance to move through whatever tough times you are experiencing. People like to think others can learn from their trials and hope others can avoid their mistakes or setbacks. It is undoubtedly a motivation propelling these others forward by sharing intimate and challenging stories. Learn from them. When you follow your light, you might then want to reach out about your experiences to others so that you can offer enlightenment!

This is the fifth anthology that resulted from *Make Your Message a Movement.* We encourage professionals and entrepreneurs to achieve their highest goals by building and nurturing relationships. One of the core philosophies is that a successful book becomes a wonderful launching pad to impact and help people with the author's life and work!

As part of our philosophy that we all need to give back to nurture and sustain human connectivity, the profits from this book are going to Kiva – an organization that helps with crowdfunding loans and unlocking capital for the underserved, improving the quality and cost of financial services, and addressing the underlying barriers to financial access around the world. Through Kiva's work, students can pay for tuition, women can start businesses, farmers can invest in equipment, and families can afford needed emergency care. Check them out on www.kiva.org.

Sit back and enjoy these five extraordinary women's heart-warming and thought-provoking stories. Their courage is contagious.

Divya Parekh and Lisa Marie Pepe

Getpublishedwithus@gmail.com

STORY 1

How to Build a Successful Business While being a Busy Mom

You need to know that your thoughts lead to your feeling, which leads to your actions, and your actions either lead to a negative or positive result.

Modupe Gbadamosi

I love dreaming, imagining things, and setting goals. I dream big to motivate myself and aspire to do great things. Dreaming is a potent brainstorming activity. It helps me to get new ideas and have some goals at the back of my mind. Such big dreams help me to work harder toward making them a reality. In my journey through life, I have had many experiences that taught me that dreaming is good. However, giving up on a dream and not achieving a goal is a total waste of time.

Most of us have dreams and aspirations. The very first time you get inspiration, the motivation is at its highest peak, and the urge to achieve is high. I realize there is a desire to achieve, but something happens along the way that holds us back. So, what could that be? What is that one thing holding you back?

The answer to this is broad and could vary from one person to the other. I will focus here on mindset, task implementation, and lifestyle alignment to answer that question. I hope my thoughts help motivate you to get over, around, or through any obstacles you encounter in making your dreams real.

Do you reflect on your beliefs, or do you ever think of what you can handle or cannot handle? What can you do to make a difference in your family's life and the next generation? I was a busy mom who had to balance those responsibilities with everything else I wanted to accomplish. You might be in the same situation or have other obligations that make it almost impossible to do what you want.

I was in that state of telling myself I was busy and had no time for myself. I had three children reasonably close together, and the best I could say is that my career was intermittent during those years. Adding to the fact that I live in a country different from where I was born and raised, you could imagine that. There's no sibling around or parents or grandparents that could help with a few errands. I returned to work when my first child was ten months old, and then more breaks occurred with the birth of the second and third. Thank God my husband had a stable job and career!

As a mom, the feeling of being overwhelmed was continually increasing. It was my daily routine to wake up in the morning, get the lunch boxes and kids ready for school, drop them off, and zoom into my office. A few hours after getting to work, my heart was already beating as I checked the time to go pick up my kids. Then it was time to get them home, eat dinner, and prepare for the next day, and the hustle continued. I had no time to take a break to reflect on my day. I was always tired, weary, and resentful. I wondered if life was going to be like this forever! I was lost in the journey of motherhood, living the life of my children.

Four good years passed, and I couldn't wait for my third child to finish kindergarten and start school. At least they could do a few things by themselves at that age. I thought I was done with childbirth and started giving away most of the things the kids had outgrown.

Mindset

However, something happened! My body was tired and weak, and suddenly it dawned on me that I was pregnant again! Ah! Goodness! I was panicking with many thoughts rushing through my head - all the sleepless nights with the baby, changes in my body, my career, the resources needed to take care of the kids, and my future. Oh, mercy! I was sweating profusely, and I was mad at myself. At this moment, everything seems meaningless.

Nevertheless, let's fast-forward my story to a year after my fourth baby was born. Seeing the child made me radiate so much joy. I braced myself up and got out of my pity party. Rather than complaining, I started to see the good in the future. It all became a positive challenge for me. When I was young, my dad often said, "Every disappointment is a blessing in disguise." In this case, it was true for me.

I awoke from my sleep. I see that sometimes facing difficult situations and having challenges is a good thing that could birth your growth and development. I became intentional with my life and wanted to find myself. I began to learn to love myself. For me, loving myself meant developing myself.

This concept got me reading and listening to podcasts. There was a particular podcast that I soaked myself into at the time. It was *Do It Scared* by Ruth Soukup. Whether cleaning, washing, driving, or even eating, I dove deep into it. At the same time, I was reading a book that opened my eyes to online business titled *What if It Does Work Out* by Susie Moore. I made a conscious effort to find time to do this reading and listening, and that was the beginning of my business success.

I soaked myself in learning through reading, taking courses, and finding good coaches that could guide me in the right direction. I realized I could achieve whatever I desired if I was willing to act toward my vision. Investing in myself became a second life for me. Not just investing in the learning of business but also learning to build relationships with myself, knowing myself, and even understanding what I thought I could not do. All these started with my mindset that I needed to believe in myself. I saw that if I lacked confidence in myself and doubted myself, I couldn't do much, couldn't impact much, and couldn't go far. Knowing yourself brings out your confidence. Investing in yourself establishes your successful future and that of the next generation.

In the beginning, I took imperfect actions. I know I had a dream, and I knew that there's a talent, a gift, a calling, and a purpose in me that needs to impact my world. But I still needed to take action to make these a reality. Mothers, can you relate? What is that gift in your hand that you have not used? That gift is your purpose. So, use it. Go after your dreams fearlessly and with conviction. I learn to feed my mind with abundance and radiance.

You need to know that your thoughts lead to your feelings, which lead to your actions, and your actions either lead to a negative or positive result. You will see the impact of your business on what you think, what you believe, and what you do.

Who does not want love, riches, influence, connections, and money? Oh yes! I love all these. I am not strange. And who doesn't like good things? All of these are great and powerful! Unfortunately, it may be the other way around if you do not know it exists in you and if you do not make use of it.

The dream in you is not as big as the power of taking action to realize the vision. Boom! I say it again! The real deal is the power of taking action to put your dream in full gear. I have seen motivation wear off if a person does nothing. Doubt and fear set in as time goes on, and eventually, the dream may not come to fruition. I challenge you, therefore, to take action.

The first action is to start to work on it now! Act on achieving your dreams! I know it's not always easy to make changes in your life, but I can tell you it's worth it. If you are a busy mom that wants a successful business, put a plan in place and set your goal for a year. Make your intentions clear. Carve time out of your busy schedule, even if it is one or two hours a day. Even working 30 minutes a day could make a huge difference. You will make the time if you want. I call it office hours. It is a special time dedicated to working on your side hustle. It is always possible only if you believe. It could take a while, but I tell you, it is doable.

Implementation

To succeed in life, you need to start somewhere. No one has it all figured out. Successful people have fear, doubts, anxiety, and worries. They just don't let these feelings stop them. Successful people act immediately when an idea or inspiration strikes their minds. The picture may not be perfect. It may not be complete. It may even be crazy. But taking action creates more motivation for continuation.

You will probably say, "Modupe, you don't understand. I don't have the time to start. I am a busy mom. I am working, and I am tired. I don't even know if I can do it. So, I will have to wait for the right time."

Do you know what? There's no such thing as the right time; there's nothing like a perfect time! For me, I had to start something I was not ready to do yet. I had to tell myself I was ready. The ideal time may never come if you are waiting for it. The secret I need you to understand is that getting started may be challenging and exceedingly difficult, but the commitment to taking action eases the progress.

So, how long will you be thinking, dreaming, waiting, and planning to start at the perfect time? I have been there! I know how it affected me. The result is bad! Bad! Bad! There is always resistance in us to start something new. Your brain will tell you to think more, see this, see that, wait, and procrastinate. The final result is that you never start! The inspiration and idea become dead. That's sad!

Remember, the people you relate with, the books you read, and what you see impacts your thoughts. Those thoughts affect your feeling, which leads you to an action to get a particular result. I have heard it said, "Taking no action is also an action." So, what thoughts are in your mind for that action?

I need to buttress here that when you start taking action, you will definitely receive some feedback, and that helps you to gradually get clarity over what you are doing. This means you are indirectly doing a SWOT analysis. (SWOT is strengths, weaknesses, opportunities, and threats). That is what leads us to love ourselves.

Be Yourself and Love Yourself

As moms wearing many hats, we always have an unending to-do list. Building a habit that prioritizes things is essential. It lessens how overwhelmed we feel. It all starts with knowing yourself. Cultivating a healthy and radiant lifestyle will help you a lot.

What do you think of yourself? Remember that the way you treat yourself is how others will treat you. Loving yourself and treating yourself as necessary is not selfish. Making it a lifestyle will be a game-changer. Self-worth is vital to your happiness and success as a business mom. It is difficult for others to see otherwise if you don't feel good about yourself or don't love yourself. Even though people could have a particular opinion about you, know that when you believe in yourself and are content with yourself, you need not convince anyone or need any approval to love yourself. So, prioritize yourself! When you are healthy, you can be capable and available to build a business of worth, even without leaving your loved ones behind.

Please feel free to use these five tips:

1. Understand that it is not what you have but what you are! It is not the resources that are available to you right now. It is what you are willing to do with your skills and knowledge, not money.

2. Embrace yourself and love yourself irrespective of the way others describe you. Believe in yourself and know that you have what it takes. We all start somewhere.

3. Stop criticizing yourself by comparing yourself to others. Do not compare the journey of the person that started 20 years ago to the one you started last year. You will get there if you refuse to give up on yourself.

4. What you are focusing on is what you are paying attention to. If you are paying attention to scarcity, you will often experience scarcity. And if you are positive and believe more in abundance, it will easily be attracted to you. So, focus on what will boost your excitement or motivation to move faster and ignore the negatives. You are responsible for your future. Nobody will change

your life for you. Stop thinking about the past, stop the blame, and be accountable for yourself and your life. You may have lost things in the past. Don't stay there; recovering is your responsibility. Focus on the positives.

5.   Prioritize what is important to you. Another thing that I want to mention is to get your intention clear. My tip here is to list out all your to-do tasks. Look through it and prioritize which one comes first. Decide to do the number one priority, delegate the rest, and leave those that do not serve you.

Surround yourself with like minds and learn to ask. Ask, ask, and ask! As I mentioned earlier, you do not have to get it all figured out at the beginning; ask people who have done what you desire to do to hasten your journey. There are unending opportunities everywhere if only you can see them. Imagine it, see it, and take it. It's your creation! God has given us all things. We have to accept them. Take it! As a busy mom, your children are watching you. They need you to be healthy and strong - mentally and physically. They see your hard work and passion and are modeling themselves after you. Make the right choice with your time.

Success will be your sweetest revenge on those who underestimate your capabilities. There is always something to learn from failing. Don't wait for a pity party. Pick yourself up and keep trying till you succeed. You have more personal power than you realize, so do not be scared of taking personal control of your life. Remember also to invest in genuine people, such that they can give you positive criticism to build you up. We do not know it all. Others can see our qualities that we cannot even see in ourselves. You can always say "no" to things that are detrimental to you. Nobody else knows best for you except you! Don't forget - you have all it takes when God is on your side. Of course, it could be scary, but remember to give yourself the grace to pause when things get in your way. After all, we are human!

Priority & Alignment

To align means putting things in the correct position in a straight line. In addition, aligning our priorities to our busy lifestyle will lessen how overwhelmed we feel. So, as a busy mom wanting to create a successful business, it is critical to position our goal, word, and life.

Goal alignment:

The goal for a business mom is to excel in business and effortlessly live a life of purpose. Make a 5-year goal plan and work with the end in mind. Break the 5-year goal into annual goals, the yearly goals into months, and months into weeks. Taking small actions over a period will lead you to the result. I recommend that you find out about the power of a vision board. It will help you. Do not underestimate the power of small steps. Actions bring clarity; clarity brings confidence, which leads to achievement. Taking action rather than thinking helps you to know whether something will work for you in your business or not. This action gives you feedback to fine-tune your work, which builds confidence in you that your work is working. Rushing to make it to the top with no direction leads to nothing. You need clarity about whatever type of online business you want to go into. Clarity breeds direction. Be clear on your goal!

Word Alignment:

I am intentional about the words I speak to myself, my family, and my business. No negative comments are allowed around me. Though I am not making millions in my business now, I will surely get there if I refuse to give up. Though I may not know everything about social media, I can learn and gradually get the hook of it. I may be scared of making videos, but I will try to do it anyway, even in imperfect ways.

Do you notice that I do not put "but" in those sentences? "But" negates and degrades! Your willingness will take the "but" away. I will not let my words tear me down; they will build me up. Words have power, and words are life. How much do you believe in the words that you speak? Does your word align with the thoughts in your mind? This is where a lot of people get affirmation wrong. It is not just speaking or saying the words; it is believing and having conviction in them. The words you speak make or break your business. So, speak life.

Life Alignment:

Life alignment, I will say, is the key to happiness. It is a transformational journey of intentionality to create a life of power, fulfilment, and purpose in your life. My life transformation started at the time I was going through challenges. It was the time I learned about self-awareness and self-discovery. I was in search of me to start the growth journey. Your obstacle, challenge, and adversity might be the great precursor to your life transformation. Whatever pain, mistake, or struggles you have gone through in life, decide not to stay in that lane by blaming anyone. Be conscious that the recovery of your success is your responsibility.

I am saying this because I have allowed others to decide for me how I should live my life. I allowed others to drive the seat of my life. I was doing things for others to feel happy and satisfied, but I was wrong that they were never satisfied. Rather, I felt a sense of dissatisfaction that led me to self-discovery. I had to take responsibility for myself, starting with a slight change. Things I used to accept that did not serve me; I stopped accepting them. I disregarded what people expected of me and deliberately focused on what pushed me to my life's purpose.

I am so glad I went through those challenges. Otherwise, I would remain in the same spot. I tell you, it is never too late to start that transformation. It all begins with discovering who you are and what you want for your life. Control what you can and accept who you are. Be grateful for your life - that you are still alive today. Reading this book means there is hope, which leads us to gratitude.

Gratitude:

Gratitude allows you to get more beauty into your life. Gratitude, when practiced correctly, will give you more joy. Radiate in the frequency of gratitude for everything and every moment. Some people secretly wish for the life you are living secretly.

Hey, Mom, are you in a business that is not working, have unstable health, or going through a relationship that is draining? I get it. You are still alive. Reading this means there is hope! Therefore, I encourage you to be grateful for the moment. If you look deep within and ignore the negatives and the complaints, there is always one thing to be thankful for. Whether you are starting or have been in business for some time, be grateful for every stage of your life. Gratitude breeds more gratitude.

Where Am I Now?

My transformation and thriving business journey started when I realized who I am and what I can do. I had a rough and unstable trip at the beginning but what helped me was that I watched the people ahead of me. I allocated time to tasks and prioritized what moved me and my business forward. I can help you too. If you are ready to invest in yourself and build a thriving business, start here.

What Can You Do Now?

Decide on your business goal. What do you know? What can you teach, or what value can you add to others willing to pay you? Brand yourself and your business on that - branding is not just about your color, font, or style; it is what you as a business stand for and how you can help your audience to achieve something or solve a particular problem. The next thing is to decide on a marketing system – ideally, an all-in-one marketing system is recommended. Systeme is an amazing marketing system. Check it at Systeme.io. Next, get business tools in place. Tools like Asana for managing your content and products, Zoom, Canva for graphics, Mailerlite to build your audience list, and others are great. Do your homework on what tools work best for you. Try to create a routine around your business. Automate repetitive tasks as all these will lessen burnout. Burnout is real in the online world. Above all, create time for yourself. You can deliver abundance where there is sanity and calm. Selfcare creates sanity and higher productivity in your business.

What you need to do for an online business is:

1. Create monthly content for your audience- create solutions to their problem

2. Create a small product to start with- sell them the solution

3. Learn to promote yourself- through relationship building.

How do you promote yourself? It is by showing up and willing to help others with your knowledge and expertise. Doing this builds more confidence in you and increases your visibility to your audience. Remember that in doing this, you are building a relationship with your audience and giving relevant value that will help them in their life and business. Everything about building a successful business boils down to these two principles. Building a relationship and providing values. This is how I started, and people are asking me for one-on-one coaching to build their businesses. My group coaching program is starting gradually. This will create more time for me, better results for my clients, and more financial success. You can do it too.

Here is a small gift for you to start taking action. Get this goal planner.

Conclusion

If you want to build a successful business as a busy mom, it may not be easy initially, but it is possible. Start with believing in yourself. Prioritize yourself and your total well-being. Be clear about what kind of business you want to build by starting to take small, consistent actions and see the momentum build. Believe me; it is never too late to start now, irrespective of age.

You can book a one-on-one connection call with me on my meeting link.

Modupe Gbadamosi is the founder of Effortless daisy – and effortless mompreneur community specially created for overwhelmed moms who are interested in building a thriving business without leaving their loved ones behind. Effortless Mompreneurs are not about making less effort but about managing & maximizing our time and resources on our priorities to build a thriving business.

Contact me: effortlessdaisy@gmail.com or dupetitilayo@yahoo.com.

And you can join us on our Facebook page and on Instagram

STORY 2

Intimacy = In To Me I See

Rising from the ashes and learning the valleys are just valleys. Death is only a shadow, and life is on the other side.

Rev. Linda Ledbeter

I was naïve. I didn't know it then, but I do now. What does it mean to walk through the valley, the shadow of death? We hear this passage so often at memorial services. In the deepest of depressions, curled up in a ball of despair, just above my right ear, I heard, "You are walking through the valley of the shadow of death; fear nothing because I am with you."

I lost my church home, my purpose, and my passion all went up in flames over lies. Church leaders covering up for those who have money and power were mind-boggling. I was sure the ministers would do what was right, but they did not. I was naïve, and I was paying the price.

A small going away party was the common practice for staff leaving their position for an easy transition. This was not afforded to me due to national church functions, and the parishioners were not given an explanation for my resignation. Furthermore, I was informed that it was against the rules for me to have any interaction with them.

The rumors began to spread, and a feeling of being a ghost among an eight-hundred-member church that was once my family was a crushing blow. People I once considered friends looked over, around, and through me:

The air was sucked out of my lungs, legs weak and unsteady. The physical pain in my heart was undeniable. I was speechless, embarrassed, and completely lost. Putting on a smile for others was impossible. The world as I knew it and all its contents were destroyed in a volcanic eruption of deceit; what was left remained covered in ashes for two-plus years.

Divine Timing is everything! My husband had secured new employment that required a major move. We were heading back to the country. Once again, the smell of rain flooded my sense; the sounds of singing birds that were silenced in the city rang in my ears. Green was greener, and I felt the earth beneath my feet. The rejection and deceit of those I had trusted remained brewing inside, and I was sad, so very sad, my passion lost in the flames of lies.

Curled up in a ball of injustice and anger, asking for direction on how to let it go, I heard a silent voice speak to me, "You are walking through the valley of the shadow of death; fear nothing because I am with you."

Soaking in the message, my heart felt a soothing flood of peace. This is a valley of life, and while I feel like I am dying inside, it is a shadow only! I am not alone. From that moment, I took charge, not playing the victim.

The following morning, I wrote a letter to the minister laying out the depth of my depression and how the lies had affected my family. I was rising up from the ashes and learning that valleys are just valleys and death is only a shadow, and life is on the other side. Closing the heart-felt letter and wishing her well, the peace from the night before carried me forward.

I once heard from a client that divorce is the hardest of all relationships because of the physical intimacy. I challenge that belief; intimacy is not just physical; it is emotional. Intimacy is the sharing of the deepest of thoughts and dreams; it's about heart and soul connection to a passion that is shared with others. Intimacy is trusting.

Swooping down like a raging fire with a Soul Sister's betrayal, my world crumbled into ash. Depression, hello old friend, what messages do you have for me to expose now?"

This time the valley was deeper, and the shadow meant looking at my own shadows. Our friendship ran deep; we traveled, took classes together, and laughed so hard we had to pull the car over.

When the verbal abuse began, I was in shock; I told myself that she wasn't feeling well. I made excuses, and without realizing it, I had begun playing the victim role.

It began with "You should..." statements, to criticizing everything I said or did. The attempts to defuse the situation made matters worse. "You can't talk to me like that!" I heard more than once. Defending myself was taken as a challenge.

More than two years into the verbal abuse that others were shielded from, it had taken a toll on my emotional and mental health. At my lowest point, lifting the fork to my mouth was an effort, and getting out the door and back home was a feat all its own.

At the core of my being, I knew that I had to honor and love myself more by walking away from this toxic relationship. It was the hardest stand I have ever had to make, but I DID IT. If I didn't honor myself, then why would anyone else?

Holding firm and avoiding contact with her caused turmoil within family and friends; it was suggested that I needed to accept how she talked to me for the communities sake. Why do I have to fall on the sword for the comfort of others? Why did I allow myself to be treated this way?

Repeatedly I heard from family and friends that she was feeling left behind and envious. The classes we were taking together gave me wings to fly, testing new spiritual concepts and imagining the endless possibilities; she was afraid for me and had self-proclaimed herself as my protector.

My shadow side liked following; it was safe. Others will like me, and I will fit in. My shadow side was also afraid of discovering my abilities of intuition, insights, and wisdom; it was keeping me safe, and taking classes challenged that.

The intuitive information I was receiving, I seriously thought it was written within the pages of the books we were reading. Often she would ask me in frustration where I got my information.

"It is in the book we just read."

"No, it's not; show me." She countered

She was right; it wasn't there, but I could clearly see the connection between what I had spoken to the words on the pages. My mistake, in all my wonder and joy, it didn't occur to me; I was awakening my Inner Wisdom.

Asking my shadow self, "If I had realized this earlier…would I have played it down or played stupid?"

This was a tough question, and I had better be receptive to the answer. Yes, I would have played small! I have played that role my entire life, with spurts of rebellion sprinkled in for balance.

Blaming others for what I was going through was no longer an option. A serious discussion with that woman I saw in the mirror needed to continue. As I worked at doing this, I began to see the bigger picture and forgive myself for things I had done and for forgiving others for what I perceived they did to me.

This betrayal brought out an anger that I didn't recognize. Verbal explosive temper tantrums haunted me; it was like I was barfing up all injustices I had endured. It felt like I needed two spotters and a stepstool to step up onto the curb.

Finally, one day, I said, "Jesus, if you're out there, I need help because I can't stand this. I can't stand this anger. I just can't do this anymore."

At that moment, I saw Jesus standing in my living room. I did a double-take and said, "I'm mad."

Jesus said, "You have a right to be mad."

I continued. "I can't live with this anger any more! I'm going to spread a lot of hostile stuff in the universe if I keep going on like this."

He said, "You're hurting yourself if you don't express these emotions. I have shoulders to carry your anger. Give it to me."

I said, "On one condition – If I do have an explosion, I don't want anyone around when they occur."

"Deal," Jesus said.

For the next six months, five to six times a day, emotional temper tantrums occurred, and as promised, no one was around. The anger deeply suppressed from childhood was being released. Insights into my patterns of survival and the need to be the Peace Maker suppressed my anger at the injustices. Implode or Explode? Imploding was no longer working or an option. Exploding without boundaries is dangerous and foolish.

Early into the eighth month, I noticed the tantrums were becoming fewer and less hysterical each day. I was getting ready for the ah-ha moment of a lifetime.

Several weeks later, I said, "Jesus, I'm so tired."

I heard, "Don't quit. You're almost there."

"Okay, you have kept your promise so far."

It wasn't long after that, while in the car, another explosive temper tantrum erupted. Suddenly, I said aloud, "Oh my God, I'm the one with the rose-colored glasses!!" I didn't see my part in any of this, which was the source of so much of my depression. Others in my drama were being themselves, even though I desperately wanted them to be something else. I burst into hysterical laughter and looked around to see if anyone else on the road noticed this screaming lady who was now laughing and crying hysterically behind the wheel.

In To Me, I See! That's when things started to shift. This entire time the temper tantrums allowed the suppressed little girl to voice herself freely and without judgment and to see relationships with more clarity.

Making reasonable excuses for other people's behavior and choosing my words carefully to avoid conflict or simply stop speaking was victimhood. I had slipped into the victim role by playing it safe.

Another valley, another shadow of death that needed to be released, allowing my authentic self room to play.

When asked how I help others navigate through their trauma, my response is there is no one or right way. Each is unique to their situation. People of all faiths or none at all are welcome here. It's what is in your heart and what calls your name that we build on.

Reaching out to a counselor or a trusted friend for support is important as a support network.

Looking in the rearview mirror, I could have benefited like many others needing medical support. Then mental and emotional health wasn't given the importance it is today. I recommend to anyone else going through events leading to depression and or anxiety to take action that is right for them.

Emotional trauma often leads to depression and anxiety, which can be complicated. Having been in abusive encounters and relationships, it is imperative to recognize it for what it is.

I believe that we must take responsibility for our part in the relationship dynamics. In the beginning, all we see is the harm we feel inflicted on us. Eventually, when we are ready and willing, we are able to see the bigger picture; that is when the healing truly begins. We are able to release those who forced us to face ourselves.

My passion is to help others, including animals, navigate their life experiences. My life and my work have become so intertwined that I bring to the table an eclectic set of tools and unique perspectives that can lead to insights that will amaze you.

Each person gets to partake in life experiences; we can play the victim or the victor. It is always a choice.

Rev. Linda Ledbeter is an Intuitive Spiritual Mentor, Animal Whisperer, Author, and Speaker. She assists people and animals in navigating their life experiences with compassion. Linda is an Ordained Minister and Counselor with All Light Ministries and A Course in Miracles. She serves as a Practitioner in Healing Touch for people and animals, Reiki Master, Shaman, and Mystic.

She believes and practices that every aspect of life experiences provides a teaching moment into self-awareness. Every person and animal that is/or has been in your life has a purpose. In her writings, this concept is conveyed through personal experiences and personal responsibility. Linda's life purpose has been about giving a helping hand when and where she can; one of her mottos is to simply show up and be present.

Over the course of twenty years, she has realized and embraced what it means to hear the passage we all are familiar with. "Though I walk through the valley of the shadow of death, I will fear no evil, for you are with me; your rod and your staff comfort me." Valleys are life's difficult moments, giving way to healing the shadow side of yourself, to fear not, for you will always have support.

Rev. Linda can be found at:

https://www.facebook.com/linda.ledbeter.1?sk=wall

https://www.facebook.com/thoughtfulconversationt hatawakenthesoul

Website: https://www.lightwindshealing.com

Email: lightwindshealing@gmail.com

Look for further books:

THRIVING BEYOND CRISIS; CONVERSATIONS WITH RESILIENT ENTREPRENEURS

Chapter 11 I Asked I Received I Screamed

A FOSTER DOG'S JOURNEY: HIGHLIGHTING ERNIE

Reality meets Reality, Moonbow publications and Productions, LLC Menomonee Falls, WI

To be published spring of 2023   Sacred Life Sacred Death

STORY 3

The Black Hole - Finding Purpose in the Pain

Without water, we will all die. Without our experiences, there would be no growth, success, or failure. It's all data that pushes our growth as humans. What's your water?

Theresa from Jersey

It was too much. The pain was so deep sometimes, so relentless. That black hole felt like it got deeper and deeper by the minute...by the second. It was all I could do not to disappear before people's eyes. Would today be the day?

A bus stopped exactly at 6 o'clock every day in front of my store. Would today be the day, I'd say to myself? Would today be my last day on this earth? Would I decide to disappear on the bus or in front of it? It was a ritual, a dance I played in my head over and over.

April 19, 1997 is the day that color left my life like a table stripped from the damage of wear and tear. I was forced to start over. From a dark bottomless pit, I felt like that table - stripped raw, a blank canvas forced to find my color again. My baby brother was gone. Murdered. My mud pie buddy, my friend, had died. A piece of me was stripped away, and I was lost.

Jeremy and I used to make mud pies as kids. If you found a worm inside the dirt, it was a bonus! We were buddies, only two years apart, so we were close. We had a deep connection all our lives. And now, he was gone.

The news I once liked to watch was now a source of anxiety and stress. We, as a family, had become the news. All I could think of was…we didn't want to be the news. We wanted Jeremy back! As imperfect as our family was and as fractured as we were before this devastation happened, this fractured us in such a way as a family that, to this day, we still have not been able to recover from it. My color was stripped, my rainbow was gone, and now all I saw was black and white, good and bad, ugly and pretty success and failure. I was color blind, and with that color, blindness came fierce anger that projected onto many people over many years because of the pain I harbored inside of myself. It shut my heart off from loving anything because I feared that I would lose it. I lived in fear every day. A trauma loop that took decades to break free from.

Let's return to that bus that stopped every day at 6:00.

I would say to myself as I watched it pull up that one of these days, I'm going to get on the bus and disappear, or I'm going to get in front of it and disappear. Is today the day? The day I disappear and start my life over as a new person and a new human being? Forgetting everything that reminds me of what I lost. Or is today the day I end it because my heart hurts so much? It's so dry, so thirsty for something, and in so much pain.

The black hole seemed to be sucking me in and holding me down in its vortex of darkness. The hole to escape got smaller and smaller. I didn't see any escape.

I was willing to do anything I could to stop this pain. So, I went to my doctor and shared what was happening. He recommended that I take antidepressants. I tried them. One would help for a little while, and then it would stop. One gave me more suicidal thoughts than before medication. Making me erratic and worse than if I wasn't on them at all.

I look back and honestly don't know how I survived that time of my life. I pulled it together enough to get some help in addition to the antidepressants I was taking. No friends at the time to rely on and no family at that time to talk to because no one wanted to face the facts. They all wanted to shove it in the closet and forget about it.

I didn't have anyone in my life. So, I dove into a religion to ease my loneliness and pain. That did not help! In fact, it infuriated me even more. I visited dozens and dozens of churches, and all I heard was, "I'm sorry for your loss." I felt as though the higher power didn't want me in any of those places. I was about to give up on life, on seeing a spiritual path.

Then I met Michelle, who lived a few houses down from where I lived. She invited me to come with her to church on Sunday. I finally felt like someone was listening to me and that I wasn't invisible. Upon going to church that Sunday, I met Shirley. She saw my pain so deep that she took me to her home after church for lunch. On a beautiful summer day after lunch, she laid a blanket on the grass and said to me, "sit under this beautiful tree, look up at the clouds, and just lie there."

For a second since my brother's murder, I felt a sliver of normal again, a sense of peace only for a moment, I wanted more of that feeling, but that wasn't reality.

My new reality is my life was about to change drastically. The jury selection and murder trials were going to happen, if I liked it or not. I left Shirley's home, feeling the black hole sucking me in further. I needed to do something for my life that was for Jeremy. But what?

I went back to that church for a while Until I decided my spiritual path would be one that I would follow by looking at myself and no one else, listening to me, finding me, and changing me. This would be a lifelong journey...called life.

I needed to do something for my life that was for Jeremy. But what?

So, I started "Jeremiah's" in 1997, shortly after my brother died. I needed something to throw myself into, and since Jeremy and I had always talked about a restaurant of our own together, I felt like it was something I could accomplish in this life that could pay it forward for him in some way.

Twenty-five years later, Jeremiah's and I have survived what sounds like a Mastercard commercial. A quarter of a century. I still can't believe all I have been through in my life and business, and I'm still standing. Every day you're with me, Jeremy, every single day.

Jeremiah's catering and the cooking studio are my way of giving back to you, Jeremy, and you're my purpose. In 1998, I moved into my business location in lake Hiawatha, NJ.

It was always a dream of Jeremy's for us to own something like this together. I would be the chef, and he would run the front of the house. It was always a childhood dream, and it wasn't something we would be able to do together anymore, but I decided I wanted to take him along for the ride when I started it. Our dream continues in its own way even after his death.

As I moved forward on it, I didn't let anything bother me or bog me down. I had a vision, and I wasn't going to be happy until I had that vision turned into reality. While that vision for my business has pivoted to change with the reality of the times, one lesson I have learned over and over again is to get comfortable with being uncomfortable as a business owner and entrepreneur. I made ALOT of sacrifices, rolled the dice with opportunities, and had to learn how to trust that the higher power has something pretty amazing picked out for me to give me this experience, this pain.

To make me uncomfortable in what happened to Jeremy, to make me stronger from the pain, and find purpose. After 25 years, it still isn't easy in business or life. I miss him so much.

I've come through quite a few bumps, scraps, and bruises on this journey in business and life. I'm pretty sure we all have had these, right?

I originally owned this business with my ex-husband for 16 years, but I couldn't let my business go because of a divorce. I gave up the house where my kids live and sacrificed to provide for them.

I took a chance to keep what I worked so hard for and to provide for my children. It wasn't easy, I was what felt like always on the verge of bankruptcy, but with continued perseverance and stubbornness, I moved forward to the next chapter, raising kids and surviving the business.

The beginning of my business was rough, but it literally kept me alive. Knowing that I had no option to quit my life or run away from it. Especially since the first three trials were about to start. I needed to pull my shit together while running a business and cooking; I remember so many times going to the courthouse in the morning and then going to the store in the afternoon and cooking and prepping by myself, crying, and chopping things. Working, so broken, barely holding it together, angry at the world, angry at myself, angry at everyone.

I now belonged to an elite club that NO ONE wants to be in. But my membership to it is my purpose. Something in my gut told me there's something that is supposed to come out of this, and you're supposed to do it. I still have that feeling every day; it is so strong and convicting. I'm coming closer every day to understanding and funneling the purpose. The people that have come into my life through the same circumstance as losing someone to murder was by no coincidence. To be able to connect with another human being that you've never met before but have this immediate bond to because they have been through something similar to you. It's a special club, again, one that we don't want to be a part of but learn to accept we are part of. What to do with it is a whole other story! That's how I met Shelly. Shelly had lost her sister to murder, and she was the one who got me through a lot of the trials. Just by listening to me. Thank you, Shelly, thank you for teaching me that I need to be there for others.

Shelly would come to the courthouse when she could. Sitting through three murder trials and listening to what people did to him three times? Once was TOO much. I wanted to jump across the room and strangle the little bastard that took his life, but I held it back, waiting for a higher purpose to kick in. Hurt, angry, scared, and confused were my companions every single day at that courthouse. It was the only thing I could do to support Jeremy. I was not strong enough to do anything else, but I knew I had to be there for him. They needed to be reminded of who Jeremy was; if seeing me made them uncomfortable, then I was in!

Finding purpose in this life for most people is a journey. But finding a purpose in what happened to my brother is a massive ball of tangled yarn.

If you think of the adage in the Bible that "God only gives you what you can handle," then essentially, we have all we need to thrive.

That's when I decided. Through the trial, I decided to get emotional help to get through the trials. Paying thousands of dollars out of my pocket, I didn't have; I didn't care. Debt or not, if I was going to survive first and move to thrive, I had to get my head and heart to communicate. I saw my therapist for over five years every week. Looking back, I don't believe I'd be alive today if I hadn't made that decision.

Through the darkness, the light, and the trials, no matter the pain, therapy helped me believe I could do it and that I had a purpose for my life. Although I was so fearful of everything around me, I wasn't going to let it control me. Afraid or not, I was going to start to find myself through the pain.

Fast forward to now, many years later. Surviving three murder trials, two recessions, one divorce, debt, bankruptcy, three surgeries, single mom hood, 25 years of dealing with people, and a pandemic (let's just add that in there!). I feel like a Mastercard commercial; learning to love yourself and set boundaries...priceless.

So, at the beginning of 2022, a thought hit me like a brick! I was going to be 50 in a month! I went on throughout the day into the next, thinking that I was going to be 50. Until I realized it was 2023, and I would be 50! Well, I was so freaking happy!!! I just gave myself back a year.

Something lit me on fire that cold Tuesday morning. MY ICE WAS MELTING! What was I going to do about it?

Like many surviving a pandemic, I felt connected to nothing in life at the moment; I had lost myself in WORK, not passion anymore. I wasn't going to go down that black hole that I'd worked so hard to stay out of. I wanted to feel connected to everything around me. How do I start? Where do I start?

Thinking about what I love and I'm good at, I started with what was natural to me, business and cooking. I started to dream again.

I started to network in business more and connected with people one on one. I started to take better care of myself, and in turn, I started to retrain my brain. I decided to command the room wherever I went. Hold the door for people regardless of if they say thank you or not.

With that, I finally understood Grace. And was able to start to apply it to how I behave and what I was able to change in myself. For the first time ever, I loved myself. Really loved me! This was big for me! I started to attract people whom I wanted in my life. For the first time, I felt in control of my loneliness.

When I decided to feel connected to whatever the name of the higher power is, is when my life started to pivot and change. As human beings, it can feel complicated whether it is the universe, science, the big bang, or Adam and Eve. Whatever we call the higher power, we need to believe it has beautiful amazingness for us. I started to live my life to reflect that.

I took the purpose of what happened to Jeremy and decided I wouldn't allow it to be a failure or a pain point. I was going to take this and turn it into an inspiration for other people who suffered through crime. I decided to be a voice for all of those people by authoring my story. I want to help those people who might be lost in the first steps of grief.

Help them with the struggle within and find themselves waiting for that epiphany - that moment where they start to feel like themselves again and start to get out of their grief. I want to be the voice that helps them through the stages of what happens next when their family member is murdered, and no one can give them any information. I want to be a spokesperson and an influencer who can inspire and help those people because I had no one when I went through it. I learned on my own and didn't have much support, so I found my own support. Me. I want to give that gift through what happened to Jeremy.

So much good can come out of so much bad.

Losing Jeremy made me understand many great beautiful things in my life. The first and foremost that I will always cherish as a lesson is that nobody is promised one second from now. As I write this, I'm lying on my hammock swinging and listening to the trees and the 287 traffic. Under this tree, I don't know what could happen in five seconds or ten minutes or an hour - I do not know. So, I need to make the most of every moment on this earth because my ice is melting! Our ice is melting!

As we come into this world, we also will leave this world. Don't let time pass you by. Know that there is no better time than right now to make a change in your life. Small changes done consistently equal amazing huge results. The right friends and company make that journey unforgettable and a thriving environment for growth and change. Thank you to my water; you all know who you are! We all have circumstances in our lives. Learning our purpose in those experiences is data and is crucial for our growth.

All experiences, good or bad, are all good because now you have data. My water taught me that. Thank you, Moon.

Outside my close friends, who are my water, I set out to surround myself with like-minded people. People who matched my energy. Twenty-five years provides a great deal of data. I remember the days in business when we had a fax machine, and you would have to manually input the fax numbers. It would send over our culinary specials to offices in the area. Now you've got email and text on like 300 platforms, lol; you've got your website, messenger, Facebook, Instagram, LinkedIn...... Whatever platform you use, you're on a million of them.

The progression of business was mind-blowing to me because I've seen the merge, the progression. I am a hybrid of the times. Social media has changed my thinking and my perspective in such a way that I realized that there is a platform to be heard. And I have something to say. Social Media has brought you to me in my story that you're reading today. I took a leap of faith, rolled the dice, and followed a gut feeling that my story would be heard.

I have visions/metas (goals in Spanish, as I learned last night at back-to-school night) for the future now. I had stopped dreaming for several years. When I started dreaming again, I rediscovered my future personal and business goals.

Personally, I want to author a series of books leading up to my face-to-face with my brother's murderer. Using those funds to create a national hotline for murder victims to have access to people who have experienced similar pain.

Business-wise, I wanted to do something in memory of Jeremy that's sustainable. There's going to come a point in my time where I'm no longer cooking. I want to pivot into teaching people the basics so they can feel confident in the kitchen to explore and go forward. My ultimate goal is to be the kind of teacher that teaches you the basics so that you can have the confidence to take it further.

Part of this call to action to want to help others and make a difference is the love for myself I have found. If I don't take care of myself, how can I help others? Focusing on helping others when my lifeboat is sinking is not going to help anyone until I learn how to plug the holes and feel good about myself. I've come to realize surviving is NOT what I want to be doing anymore. I WANT to thrive!

To thrive, I had to learn how to care for myself, take smaller bites in business, make a choice, and stick with it till death do I part. To thrive, I had to see color again. I felt something awaken in me when I realized this. The seed just received the water it was looking for. The data had been collected, and it was ready to be used. The seed was learning how to grow.

I have not coped well with a lot of things in my lifetime. I've made a lot of bad decisions, and I have paid the consequences of my actions many times. I have pissed off a lot of people, and I have hurt many people along the way too.

I needed to change; for me, I was ready to grow.

My epiphany was Grace! It made me think, and I wanted to apply it to my life in an instrumental way. It was just like a light bulb went off. I always call it Thomas Edison.

Grace is where my hard look in the mirror started.

At that point, I decided to love the "woman in the mirror" and be happy with her, and if she fucks up, it's ok. What are you going to learn from it? Always be looking forward to how to turn it around. One thing I realized when I started this journey was I wouldn't be fearful of speaking, getting up in front of people, or any stigmas or rejection.

I made the conscious decision that people wouldn't ignore me anymore. I was going to command the room wherever I went. I started to believe in myself and believe what my capabilities are because I've been through many, many, many storms in business, relationships, and family. To date, good or bad outcomes, I have weathered them all! I've survived the scrapes and bruises from clawing my way out of the grip of the black hole. I'm finally ready to grow!

The seed has water now, and it is starting its journey.

Ask yourself:

What is watering you?

What do you want your pain to bring purpose to?

———————～～————————

Theresa Navarro is the proud single mother of Gabriella and Alexander Navarro. "While parenting is challenging by yourself," Theresa has realized, "it has allowed a deeper bond to form with my children." *Theresa from Jersey* inspires people to look at themselves in the mirror and make a change!

Her goal in life as Theresa Navarro is to be the best version of herself, inspirer, mother, daughter, sister, and business thriver... by continuing to look at the person in the mirror and changing what needs to be changed to move forward. Theresa believes it is not easy to retrain the brain as people make mistakes. But as long as we acknowledge and accept, anyone can change. It will be a work in progress for the rest of our lives, but the result is rewarding.

On her "off" time, Theresa enjoys playing volleyball and meeting new and interesting people from all over the world.

As the chef and business owner for 25 years of Jeremiah's catering and cooking studio, chef T prepares culinary treats and parties for clients as well as cooking instruction for kids, special needs, and adults.

Whether you're looking for a catering get-together/event or wanting to gain better skills in the kitchen, chef T would love to be a part of your experience!

You can connect with Chef T at:

Theresafromjersey.com

Jeremiahscatering.com

https://www.facebook.com/groups/13219103716099 81/

STORY 4

My MS Transformation

My doctor nailed me with a look, raised his voice, and stated. "If you don't take one of these medications, you'll be in a wheelchair in 6 months."

Sylvia J. Sharp

I was in LAX after an 11-hour flight from Fiji. I had a long layover there and was so exhausted that I had crawled under benches to sleep. I was making my way to the last flight in my marathon journey home when MS (multiple sclerosis) first hit me. It began with me tripping over my left toe. I chalked it up to travel fatigue. I boarded my flight home, and approaching my seat, I miscalculated the trajectory of my bag and slugged the poor woman I had to then climb over clumsily to get to my seat. My body was not exactly under my control, and I was confused. I've always been very coordinated. I would find out later these were all symptoms of MS, but I thought it was just the extremely long travel after playing hard in Fiji.

I apologized profusely to my seatmate, but her stony silence had me crying softly and alone in my window seat. I kept telling myself, "You're just tired." I had no idea what the winter to spring semester was about to bring me or how those two little letters – "M" and "S" - would transform into the most frightening thing I'd ever faced personally. That my deep belief that life is always happening for me, a conversation with God, and a doctor mistreating me turned the whole situation around.

I had been in Fiji participating in a 10-day health seminar through Tony Robbins. In fact, I had already transformed from a size 16 to a 6 even before I took off for Fiji by balancing my PH and combining my food in a manner to simplify my digestion. I also did a simple daily walk for cardio. I learned this approach from the final day of Tony Robbins' 4-day immersive experience at the beginning of November that he calls UPW (Unleash the Power Within).

At that same event, just 2 ½ months prior, I came to the realization that through life lessons and difficulties, God transforms us. Each transformation is a gift since we as humans simply grow through challenges. If we see our challenge as a gift later, can we embrace it as a gift before the transformation? So, I was in the airport on the way home from Fiji when my "gift" showed up with my first symptoms of MS. I, of course, didn't know this at the time. I thought I had just "played" too hard in Fiji.

I continued to trip over my left toe when I returned to teaching. (In the MS community, we call this foot drop.) What's happening is that your brain is not giving a signal for your foot to rise off the floor enough, therefore, "dropping" it. A few months later, it was still happening. By now, though, I also had to lift my left leg into my car. So, I went to my doctor, who sent me to a neurologist. The doctor ordered a spinal tap, and my spinal fluid was examined.

They found that I had the "right" markers in my spinal fluid, even though "right" seemed the opposite of what was going on, but they confirmed I had MS! Multiple Sclerosis. The doctor informed me in May, the day before my last faculty recital at SUNY Fredonia, where I sang with the jazz band. I performed with fellow faculty member and friend Dr. Linda Phillips as she accompanied me while I sang in three languages and danced with my dear friend Paul W. Mockovak from the Theatre Arts faculty. As I took his hand, I wondered if it would be the last time I'd dance on a stage.

When I got home from my recital with my mother, I set my program on top of the three beautiful, high glossy magazine-quality gift boxes of information, some with videos and actual celebrity endorsements that the doctor had given me. I had only experienced this highly professional style when big money was on the line. They were clearly competing for my business. The high gloss reflections of light off of the beautiful boxes proved it. As I followed this thought to its conclusion, I realized I might be taking this medication for the rest of my life, and these companies wanted me as a long-term customer. I could tell taking their medicine was in their best interest. My question was, "Was it in mine?" Was this just big business dressed as healthcare?

As I began my research, those two little letters of MS played over and over in my head, and my fear stacked, and God forgive me; I had moments of idiocy and madness where I wished for another "get overable" disease. MS can attack you anywhere, at any time. There is no planning for it. For me, a "get it done," certainty-driven control freak, it was terrifying. And, it was a life sentence.

Just six months before, I had learned from Tony Robbins that gratitude is the solution to fear. It's a simple concept; you cannot feel these two emotions simultaneously, but how on earth was I going to manage gratitude for MS? I didn't know, but I believed I could.

Over the following weeks, I conversed with God as I walked each morning. Deeply believing that life was happening for me, I asked myself one day, "OK, what is God helping me learn from this? Would I become more courageous, valiant, loving, resilient?" Yes! Not only that, but He believes I can! The statement that life is happening for me was never more evident.

Our trials are indeed gifts. We grow and learn from them and, in overcoming them, become better and better humans. I remember this moment so clearly! As I write this, the tears come again with a flood of awe and gratitude. Thank you, God! If You think I'm up to the challenges I will encounter through my experiences with MS. I'm blown away that You think so.

With tears of gratitude streaming down my face and a vote of confidence written on my heart from my creator, my thoughts took me further to what I'd become through this "refiner's fire." This fire that fashions swords is God's refining fire that would make me a beautiful human. (Psalm 66:10) I'd genuinely get better and better. The incantations I did every morning came to mind: "Every day, in every way, I'm getting better and better!" I'd whisper-shout every morning. It was true; not just a way to pump myself up.

So, I embraced new words, "Every day, in every way, I'm more and more spectacular!" I'd become "more and more spectacular" as God worked on me. Those two terrifying letters MS now meant more spectacular! This wasn't denial because I knew I'd face more tests, but each would become a gift unlocking my further growth. I found my gratitude! I took this to mean I could serve more people better and better as I grew. To me, serving others is the best way to spend my life. I did so in Fiji later when I was part of the crew for the same program I participated in right before my diagnosis.

Before my diagnosis in Fiji, I had come to accept that no one cared more for my health than myself. Therefore, I'm in charge of my own health. My health journey was not in the hands of the doctors I went to but in my own. I also learned that when the body is experiencing flu symptoms, it is reacting to an internal situation where the body desperately needs to get rid of whatever it is by any method or orifice necessary. Whether my conclusion was right or wrong is debatable, but when I read the side effects of all of these medications (Interferons), they were flu symptoms. My mind said, "Oh, hell no!" I did not want them in me. I'd rather deal with MS symptoms than flu all the time. Keep in mind that doctors didn't yet know what causes MS. I felt if they didn't know, then this medicine was nothing but an educated guess. I didn't want to be a lab rat for the doctors' experiments.

So, a few weeks after my recital, I went back to the doctor. He was about to discover that I am a different kind of patient! When he inquired which medicine I'd be taking, I said, "None of them," I could feel the outrage radiating off him. He then nailed me with a look, raised his voice, and stated. "If you don't take one of these medications, you'll be in a wheelchair in six months." Yes, he was wrong to speak to me this way, but I praise God for him because he gave me precious gifts that day. He gave me a target for my anger and a purpose in proving him wrong. In my head, I said, "Oh yeah? Watch me!" I was furious. Within six months of harnessing my anger, I was running 16 miles a week. I hadn't run since junior high. Sometimes it's good to be mad!

Thanks to him, my research was fueled and urgent. In my research on MS and my brain, I discovered the term "neuroplasticity," which is our ability to create new neural pathways in our brain and learn. Our brains can create workarounds, but you can't be limited by what you think and insist your brain do. I basically insisted on my leg working. As I did, I started to understand the magic of neuroplasticity. I had been in marching band in school, so since my foot drop was on the left, I'd make my leg march on that side. I looked mighty strange walking down the street, but I had a fire in my belly, thanks to that doctor. I also applied this later to strength training, doing more on my left until the two sides balanced, although I had many arguments with trainers about this. So, I was marching on the left, and, eventually, I was not only physically fine, but I began running 10 yards at a time and then 20 yards. I started attaching the yards together until I was running for all of it, still using my "More Spectacular" incantation daily. Over the course of months, by the time May turned to November, I was running four miles four times a week. That is 16 miles a week.

Sometimes we need something or someone to battle against in our efforts to bring about change. It becomes a perceived injustice. MS was big, cumbersome, and even overwhelming as a target for my anger, but the doctor was a perfect foil. I was blessed to be his patient and for God to prod him to raise my anger to become my fuel. There are many wonderful doctors in this world! Listen to their advice and reflect on it, but know it's your own choice, not a given outcome, to act on or accept their advice.

I dropped my incantations along the way, one of my less-than-brilliant moves, but I'm back to doing them now after caring for my mother with dementia at home for over three years, a year by myself while managing my illness. Then after nearly two more years with my brother helping with my mother, I re-claimed this incantation.

Caring for mama was equal parts blessings to challenges. Mama's dementia was such that she didn't remember she needed a walker or that I had MS, even though she lived through my diagnosis with me. We monitored her 24/7, including her many nightly trips to the bathroom. I didn't want to undermine her delicate sense of security for our situation as two ladies living alone. So, I only explained my MS when she could tell something was off.

After her passing, when I started back with my incantations, I could only get to the end of the block and back. That took me fifteen minutes. Now, four months later, I'm starting to run during my walk just as I did before. I also have signed up for a 5K on Thanksgiving day. My deep belief that life is always happening for me continues to be a source of light to me. It helped me come up with the idea of sharing what I was learning while caregiving. I worked at growing this content, but eventually, I had to set it aside to manage mama's care better. I've been working on content ideas since she went to heaven in February 2022. I have a Facebook group for support called Champion Caregivers, not because we're so great, but because we are "champions" for our parents. The content I've produced is on Caregiver Support Community on Instagram, Facebook & YouTube, although on Facebook, it's called Caregiver Support Channel. Links to all of them can be found at www.sylviasharp.com.

During my 1st year of caring for mama, I authored a book, The Agreement. I hope it will be published close to the release of this book. It details how my mother and I came to an agreement on her care long before she needed it. It also explains how the same agreement helped her hand me her car keys at 89 when she needed to stop driving.

"For thou, hast tried us oh God; Thou hast refined us as silver and gold." (Malachi 3:2) This verse has quite a different meaning to me now. It reminds me of the Japanese traditional art of repairing pottery with gold called Kintsugi. In this discipline, the flaws and scars become a transcendent commentary on the passing of time and seeing beauty in the imperfect. It is a magical thought when I see the times life has broken me and my creator mended me with gold.

If we are left with an uneventful life, we'd never grow and become better. The Law of the universe is that things are either growing or dying; there is no standing still. I am so grateful for the person I've grown into, and I'm dedicated to growing. If you like who you are at the core of your being, you can thank your trials, as I do mine, for the growth they fostered.

What gifts were brought to you through the trials you are proud to have gone through? Is there a trial, even a small one, in your current circumstance? Consider, if we will see the gift in a circumstance later, why not embrace it now?

Sylvia J. Sharp is a former opera singer & voice teacher. She most recently occupied herself with round-the-clock caregiving for the last three years of her mother's life. The first year of this was done alone & during the onset of the Covid-19 pandemic. Her mother, Joanna K Sharp, was 99½ when she went to heaven in February 2022. They had lived together for 17 years.

Sylvia now wants to share her caregiving journey. The good, the bad, the tips, and the tricks she used to get through it all. She continues to create free social media content to support caregivers who care for aging parents at home and has a special place in her heart for caregivers with health challenges of their own.

Her email contact is customerservice@sylviasharp.com.

www.sylviasharp.com

STORY 5

Entrepreneur Under Adversity

Keep the Faith!

Linda Stapleton

My story is about faith in God because I have gone through a lot over the past few years that have reminded me how strong you need faith at times. I have experienced death, taking care of very close relatives while they were sick, and doing all of this as I've kept a thriving business going. I believe sharing my personal and business challenges can help others facing adversity in their life. You can come out on the other side! I believe it is a blessing that I have been able to take care of others and continue my business. You might have to juggle things differently than before, but you can do it.

I have been caring for my husband, who has MS (multiple sclerosis), and my sister, who has been going through a series of health issues. However, the story begins when my mother passes away. I thought my whole world was going to end because my mom was everything to me, and she still is. I go to the cemetery to visit her every weekend to sit and talk with her. We made a garden for her at the gravesite because she loved plants and loved to garden.

Our bond was one that I didn't think would ever be broken. The day she passed away was when I thought everything around me came to a grounding halt. It was an extremely hard pill to swallow, and I am not sure that I have swallowed it yet.

She passed away about a month before the Covid pandemic hit us and shut down the world. It happened before the 2020 Super Bowl when the Kansas City Chiefs won the big game. My family all gathered for that game as we are remarkably close. We were all at my mom's house for the Super Bowl - the children, the grandchildren, the great-grandchildren, the great-great-grandchildren. It was five generations at her place, and it was so appropriate that the Chiefs won, as my mother loved the Kansas City Chiefs and Patrick Mahomes. It was so right, as if her spirit was right there with us.

We were at the hospital the day she died because it seemed my mother had a major heart issue. She was wearing Patrick Mahomes #15 jersey, and the doctor said, "We're going to have to cut her clothes off and get her into surgery right away."

My mom looked at the doctor and nurses and said, "I just bought this shirt!" She was laughing at the situation, just as she did with so much. She didn't seem to be in much physical distress other than sweating a lot when she arrived, even though the doctors thought she had a massive heart attack.

As she was laughing and talking, I told her, "Mama, let them cut it off. I'll buy you another one. Don't worry."

She asked, "What time are you going to do this surgery?"

When told they would take her up right away, I said, "You know I love you," and kissed her. "We'll be right here when you come out."

She never came out.

It was heartbreaking, to say the least. She was always a graceful woman, and she left gracefully, too. She was a beautiful person inside and out. When she died, the entire city was in shock because my mom knew many people, as did my family. It was the worst thing that could possibly happen. I now know that if I can handle that, I can handle anything

As for my husband, John, he was already having some health issues, and doctors had already diagnosed the MS. Multiple sclerosis is a disease that impacts the brain, spinal cord, and optic nerves, which make up the central nervous system and controls everything we do. However, it didn't get bad until the past few years.

Everybody thinks my husband looks like Barack Obama. They even have the same mole on their nose. He's an older version of Barack. He started to lose weight. But, it has been one thing after the next. He lost his eyesight and other physical abilities. He has a lesion on his brain and is not as strong as he was.

Besides my husband, I am also taking care of my sister Cheryl. She had back surgery and a hip replacement after the back repair. She needed a great deal of help after the operations. Every four hours, I had to be up to get her medication if she was in pain or to get her back and forth to the bathroom. I had to do everything for her. She has her own home but can't live on her own quite yet. At the time of this writing, she'll probably be with me for another six months or so.

At one point, she thought she was strong enough to drive herself to a doctor's appointment. I asked her if she was sure and then advised starting with some short trips – like going to the store and back. When she was doing well with this, I thought she was okay to go to the doctor's office.

Well, I was at the office and had clients with me. I got the phone call that she was there, but she blacked out! Oh, my goodness! By the time I got to the hospital, they had put cold water all over her. The doctors weren't sure why it happened, but I was watching her very closely. She is undergoing more tests, and hopefully, we'll find out what's going on with her. It's always a challenge.

As you can imagine, running the business my husband and I owned got exceedingly difficult. Because John sometimes can't get out of bed and can't walk, I had to close the downtown office of our business. We were working together in the Northland office, but we had to close that office because things got even worse for John. Our business is centered around personal injury and worker compensation cases. John authored many books and gave seminars on workers' compensation. He's traveled for the Missouri bar all over the country. John knew worker compensation law backward and forwards.

After he was diagnosed with MS and it got worse, we slowly had to start closing offices. I finally moved to a much smaller office about five minutes from my home because I

might need to get back to the house at any moment. Now, I don't take as many cases as I used to, and I'm trying to move from the practice of law to restorative justice, which is much easier to administer. It doesn't have all the research and craziness you must do when working on personal injury and worker compensation cases.

Restorative justice is an approach to justice that seeks to repair harm by providing an opportunity for those harmed and those who take responsibility for the harm to communicate about and address their needs in the aftermath of a crime. The interconnected concepts of encounter, repair, and transformation are the three core elements of restorative justice. Each element is discrete and essential. Together they represent a journey toward well-being and wholeness that victims, offenders, and community members can experience. With so many problems that we're having in our world, restorative justice is necessary as it's needed everywhere. There are civil, criminal, juvenile, and employment cases everywhere. It's definitely needed.

As an example, we had a problem at one of the outstanding school districts in my area where they were sending a petition around telling kids to sign it to bring slavery back! We helped bust that up, and it looks like it is over. So, we try to offer restorative justice wherever we see something like that happening. Unfortunately, it happens almost every day, whether it's in the school system or at the workplace. There's a definite need for such an effort.

In fact, before my husband got extremely sick, we began putting together a curriculum for college students. We have two years of curriculum put together already to offer as a course in a college setting on restorative justice. We had to slow down a little bit and didn't move forward with it. We still have it, and we're ready to move far with it when John gets a little better than where he's at now.

To show you the impact of our work, we had someone come to us who had been in prison for 27 years. The police found the actual perpetrator of the crime, and the courts granted him freedom. The man was very gracious but felt he should receive compensation for those years. There are so few programs in prison to help someone who committed a crime to become a better person, and there was certainly nothing to help someone in his situation. We were able to help him to some extent.

Then there are the kids in juvenile court. I sat on the executive board at Kansas, Missouri Juvenile Justice Center. I've been on that board for more than 25 years. I have seen many kids repeatedly come through the courts' doors. You can help these kids if you connect with them correctly.

Restorative justice is something we've applied to some of these cases where kids are committing a crime or being disruptive in school. If you can stop them from acting this way at an early age, you don't get that recidivism when they become adults.

One boy was always making jokes and talking about other people. He was getting into trouble all the time because he did not know how to read. He wanted to learn but would instead bully people all the time and get in trouble. Instead of the school deciding to help him and find out what was going on, they would rather suspend him for ten days. We came across the situation and decided to find out what was going on with this kid. He was 12 years old, and as it turned out, he needed someone to care about him.

I found this out by talking with him. I started instilling into him the love that I felt for him. I wanted him to know that somebody cared about his success. I found out he grew up without a dad, which is tough for anyone. I gave him my cell number and told him he could call anytime to talk. I told him that if he felt like he was getting ready to make a bad decision, he should call me. Sometimes I would call him simply to ask how his day was going. He was totally shocked by this! He said no one had ever done that with him before.

I believe I touched his heart, and he started to change. After a while, I asked him what books he liked. He would tell me, and I asked him if he wanted to go and get that book. We'd go to the library or Barnes and Noble. I'd give him the book as a gift and tell him to let me know what he thought about it after he read it. Sometimes we'd read it together.

He turned out to be a great kid and did learn to read. I still talk to him today. It doesn't matter where you come from; it is a matter of how people treat you and you treat them.

Then there was a woman going through therapy because she had been in a bad marriage. I talked with her one day and gave her some good things to listen to that would help her. I believe she was appreciative that someone to the time to actually listen! She told me, "Linda, I have been seeing a therapist for the last two years, and I've learned more coming here in the last two weeks than I've learned in the last two years. I want to thank you for that."

Of course, it felt good to hear this. She got up enough courage to divorce the man abusing her for all those years. I have a mother-in-law's quarters in my home, but I never used it. I welcomed this woman to come and live in my home because it has its own private entrance and everything, and it's completely separate from the living space in my home. It was a safe place after all the physical and mental abuse she had absorbed. She stayed there for about ten months; it helped her to prepare to move on with her life.

I must admit that with this kind of work and taking care of John and Cheryl, I would like to take a month off and sleep. Unfortunately, I don't have that luxury. I can't be down. For the most part, I never even think about those things because I know it's not going to happen any time soon.

My strength comes from believing that God made me in the image and likeness of Christ.

You cannot be sick, hurt, or afraid. So, I always try to manifest my true self. God said everything he made is good. I believe that, and my struggles don't phase me as long as I keep that truth at the front of my mind.

To anyone reading this, I say to love yourself, have faith in God, and keep moving.

Stay hungry and stay focused on the things that matter in life. I'm not talking about material possessions here!

People remain too focused on material things. They forget we are born into this world with nothing. Whatever we accumulate, we're not going to die with them. Nothing that we have is going with us. You can't take your BMW or Mercedes with you. Thus, it would be best if you focused on the spiritual essence of life.

I can remember when I was a young kid, and I saw this car. I said, "Oh, my God! When I grow up, I'm gonna buy that car. It's beautiful." It was a Cadillac Eldorado. In my little diary, I wrote the year, the name, and everything about that car. Of course, when I got old enough and started looking for the car, it looked like a piece of junk. I did end up buying one, but it was a lesson that you can't say I'm going to be happy when I get this or that because it all turns to rubbish at some point. We are not going to be here forever. Everything is just on loan.

It's like when my mom was here. I had purchased a really beautiful condo that she fell in love with, and she wanted it. So, I said, "Okay, I'll get it for you." I did, and then, after she passed it, it was time to let it go because it was just not good to go there since she was not with me. It was time to let it go, so I sold it and received double what I paid for it.

You are happy when you take care of other people. That's what God wants us to do. He wants us to help people. It is like the story of the Good Samaritan, where two people pass by a hurt man without helping him. The third person was not much of a friend to the injured man's people, but he stopped and helped him anyway. So, don't walk past anyone that needs your help. You have to stop and say, "Are you okay? What can I do to help you?" You have to love your neighbor as you love yourself, and sometimes I love my neighbor more than I love myself.

When you get the challenges in life like I have had, you have to decide that you must do what you have to do. You know, it's not a coincidence that God happened to say, "Okay, here's your husband who's going to be sick. Here's your sister. You're going to have to take care of these things." He knows to whom to give those responsibilities and that you can handle them.

You can't complain but have to say, "Thank you. Lord, thank you. I appreciate that you trust me to handle these things, and I will do the best I can with every fiber of my being because I know that you don't give people more than what they can handle."

Please take that lesson from my experiences and run with it. "Keep moving," as my mother always said. Don't complain because, by the time you finish complaining, you could have had ten things done by then. You know that God has chosen you to handle things and gave you the strength to do it. That is a great blessing in itself.

Linda R. Stapleton has been CEO of Midwest ADR and Legal Administrator of the Stapleton Law Firm for the last 20 years. She has extensive experience in personal injury and unusual and innovative worker's Compensation cases. Her recent activity and passion include Restorative Justice and Mediation. She is an author of over 20 books as a result of her passion for helping others when she is not preoccupied with her daily work at Stapleton & Associates, LLC. Linda also has a great love for her family, with whom she loves spending quality time every week. Linda has

served on a number of Boards. She currently serves on the Executive Board for Children's Emergency Fund at the Juvenile Court in Kansas City, Missouri, where she has volunteered for more than 20 years helping juvenile offenders see a better life for themselves. Another Board that is most important to Linda is the Lecture Board for Christian Science Lecture Committee. Linda's greatest passion is bringing healing to people who have been through a traumatic or stressful experience, which includes children, adults, and families, to find healthy perceptions of themselves so that they can know themselves as peaceful, complete, whole, and safe.

Linda R. Stapleton's educational background includes a JD in legal studies, a BA in Psychology, and an Associates in Business Administration. Additionally, Linda has several certificates in various studies and is now working on a Masters of Theology at Grand Canyon University in Phoenix, AZ.

You can connect with Linda at:

www.midwestADRKCLLC.com

Email: Linda@slfstapletonlawfirm.com

Will You Leave a Book Review?

Did you enjoy this book and find it helpful?

We will be very grateful when you post a short review and give your success story on Amazon right now!

Your support makes a difference. In addition, we read and respond to all the reviews personally to make this book even better!

To leave a review right now, go to www.amazon.com.

About The Art of Unlearning Founders

Divya Parekh, a 10-time #1 bestselling author, business growth strategist, and motivational speaker, partners with high-achieving business owners, experts on the rise, Fortune 500 leaders, and Fortune 50 leaders who are ready to play full out, experience the joy of impacting others, and expand their reach, business, and revenue.

Together, they build power positioning and recession-proof business through simplifying, strategizing, and scaling the business. In addition, Divya supports first-time and published authors to turn their unique message into an inspiring movement. She does this by helping them communicate their message through business-focused and personalized book writing. This approach, in turn, positions them as industry leaders, accelerates business growth, and increases business profits. Divya's #1 best-selling books, including her Expert to Influencer: How to Position Yourself for Meaningful Impact and The Entrepreneur's Garden – The Nine Essential Relationships to Cultivate Your

Wildly Successful Business, prove that her concepts reap huge rewards. Divya and her team have helped more than 170 authors implement their vision, become #1 bestselling authors, and garner six-figure opportunities.

Divya is committed to helping people move through the transformational journey of becoming influential leaders for the rest of their lives! Divya's books and strategies have been endorsed by the likes of Brian Tracy, Marshall Goldsmith, Kevin Harrington (Original Shark from *Shark Tank*), James Malinchak (ABC's *Secret Millionaire*), Sherry Winn (Two-time Olympian), and many more…As a thought leader, she regularly contributes to prominent publications like Forbes, Entrepreneur, CEO World Magazine, Addicted to Success, and International Coaching News. Divya has also been a radio personality and host for the past five years on multiple platforms.

https://entrepreneur.divyaparekh.com/

Please accept my Free Gift:

"Get Started in A Week-Business Book Writing" Challenge

Friends, I get a lot of great questions from clients and people about how to get started to write a book in a faster way— without adding stress and a ton of extra hours to their plate. The questions arise because 81% of people have a book in them. Few ever finish. If you believe that you have a message that will impact others, then I know that your book is needed. Many people are doing things in a way that are…cumbersome, time-consuming, overwhelming, and more complicated than they need to be. So, I've decided to create a No-Cost and Low Effort 5-Day Challenge to help you, a person who wants to share their message, make an impact and amplify profits.

Join the few and become an author. It's not that hard. I'll walk you through it in a simple, five-day "Get Started in A Week-Business Book Writing" Challenge at your pace and in the comforts of home.

https://success.divyaparekh.com/5daywritingchallenge

Lisa Marie Pepe The Confidence Coach and Online Visibility Expert for passionate, heart-centered women entrepreneurs, a #1 International best-selling author of The Art of Unlearning: Top Experts Share Conscious Choices for Empowered Living, and a motivational speaker.

Trained at the graduate level in both Education and Clinical Psychology and with over three years of experience as a successful virtual assistant and social media manager, Lisa Marie empowers her clients to fully embrace their unique gifts and talents by providing them with the skills they need to develop rock-solid confidence and become vibrantly visible online.

She has been featured in The Huffington Post, Thrive Global, YFS, and several other noteworthy publications. Lisa Marie has also appeared as a special guest expert on over 40 international tele-summits and has been interviewed on dozens of highly regarded podcasts such as The Stellar Life, The Big Movement, and Women in Leadership.

Lisa Marie is available to speak on self-empowerment, overcoming obstacles, confidence building, positive psychology, entrepreneurship, online business growth and development, and online visibility strategy.

Please accept my Free eBook:

6 Ways to Amplify Your Online Visibility

In this guide, you'll receive step by step instructions, tips, tricks, and strategies on how to best: Share Your Social Media Links Be Consistent and Congruent on Social Media Use Customized Hashtags on All Your Posts Repurpose Your Facebook Livestreams Optimize Your Facebook Business Page Use Automated Response Apps ... all so that you can AMPLIFY YOUR ONLINE VISIBILITY!

https://positivetransformationlifecoaching.leadpages.co/6-ways/

www.ingramcontent.com/pod-product-compliance
Lightning Source LLC
Chambersburg PA
CBHW070527030426
42337CB00016B/2143